MUSIC'S BRIDE

Also by Marius Kociejowski

DOCTOR HONORIS CAUSA

MARIUS KOCIEJOWSKI

Music's Bride

ANVIL PRESS POETRY

Published in 1999
by Anvil Press Poetry Ltd
Neptune House 70 Royal Hill London SE10 8RF

This book is published with financial assistance
from The Arts Council of England

Designed and set in Fournier by Anvil
Printed and bound in England
by Cromwell Press, Trowbridge, Wiltshire

ISBN 0 85646 318 3

A catalogue record for this book
is available from the British Library

for my parents

ACKNOWLEDGEMENTS

Acknowledgements and thanks are due to the following periodicals in which some of these poems first appeared: *Agenda*, *Babel*, *The Jerusalem Review*, *PN Review* and *Sakura*, and two anthologies: ... *as the case requires* (printed for Dennis Andrews, 1994) and *The Old Enchanter: A Portrait of George Johnston* (Penumbra Press, 1999).

'Dinu Lipatti plays Chopin's Sonata in B minor' and 'The Charterhouse at Valldemosa' were published together in a limited edition entitled *Sonata and Prelude* (Ulysses, 1999).

CONTENTS

PART ONE

Tiger Music

'You see that eminence?
You shall have your heart's fill of them there.'
The village elder, almost blind, pointed to a crag floating
in distant haze.
Thus sped with hope,
Our guns cocked, although it never was our purpose to kill,
we went looking for tigers.

If what the *fellâhîn* said was true,
If there was nothing they could not, in their language,
describe,
We met not a soul who knew all the words, the more than
fifty or so,
That speak the many shades of tigerness between one
which dozes
And another that lunges,
the different music they make.

All day we watched for movement in the stone.
We saw lizards which at our approach slid off like lightning
into crevices.
A couple of eagles from an eyrie
on the crag above
Wheeled and hovered, their shadows like two
Spots of ink moving upon the mountain-side.
We watched for tigers but saw none, although we did see
A gazelle, its gashed throat jewelled with flies.

Whiteness pooling his eyes, the village elder
was confused or so he appeared.
'What could have made them go away?' he asked. 'Once,
I saw tigers everywhere.'

All night we fought among ourselves.
One man said leopards dwelled here, while another lynxes.
Anything but tigers, such was the consensus of all but one.
The old boy stuck to his guns, of course, warned us
Of the dangers that come of grabbing tigers by the tail.
'A snake doubles back upon half its length,' he said,
'whereas a tiger goes it whole.'
Our dragoman, scoffing at him, said this was
A country as bare of tigers as his soul of truth.
'So why, then,' the other replied, 'if indeed there are none,
Should our language have fifty or more words for the many
moods they strike?'
We drank our bitter coffee,
And discussing what provisions we should take,
Said tomorrow perhaps would see the settlement of our
dispute,
As to what those famous tigers really were.

A Seventh Jew

E lucevan le stelle . . .

A darkness such as this he can almost taste.
What else?
Smell, oldest of memories, he smells her fragrance.
And what else? At the end of a garden path sounds of a
creaking gate,
A patter of footsteps that makes heart leap like a hare,
Almost too fiercely for its slender cage.
Anything else?
Yes, he who has never loved life so much as he does now
Covers with kisses the nakedness of her face, sings as he
would before a heavenly judge.

We owe him so much more than just our lives,
This Jew from Lyon who, if only he had trained his voice,
Might have made, if not the big rôles, then operetta perhaps.
Still, there's no saying what in odd circumstances a beginner
will do,
As when he learns this may be his only chance
And the one whose part he sings is about to die.

We imagine just how it was,
Seven men pushed down the corridor's bright glare to the
courtyard beyond,
As if allowing them to go in peace would destroy the
bigger scheme
Which was to make men less than what they are.

The names of six survive.
Of the seventh, the anonymous one, we know only he was
a Jew with a fine voice,
Who, from behind bars, made true a certain woman's
perfume,
A meeting at dawn beside a garden gate.
What is any history of resistance, if not this voice tender
Yet strong enough to remove from other men's ears
extraneous noises,
The squeaking of boots, a key scraping in the hole.
As he sang whose face did he smother with kisses?
So finely registered was this performance, so pure his
timbre,
Somebody there simply had to take note.

Full Force

i.m. Christopher Whelen

1

We watch as they warmly embrace,
This couple we think of as foes.

We must let them pass unhindered.
We must keep from them our applause,
As they reckon what joggles the spirit is worth double
What smarts behind the eyes.

They walk along the downward path,
Speaking of all things small rather than large.
The pebbles are sometimes loosened,
And rush ahead like smooth heralds.

2

They breathe deeply the crop of late,
And there beneath the harvest moon push as one
Through the turnstile of speech.
We must spend shrewdly their silence.

The stars have come out in full force.

The old bruisers standing in the middle
Of the field study them until their necks begin to ache.
They grow heavy with fatigue, for
Although their hearts are open wide
Their minds are sealed against the infinite as against death.
They are at too tender an age.

We watch the slight, bent silhouettes,
Almost clownish, as they trudge home.

A Pavane for Sydney Housego

When Sydney fiddles, Bach fumes in his grave.
Mojo whines.
Mojo, ears bigger than his master's, listens to the music of the spheres,
Which is why when Sydney scrapes at the violin he drops snout between paws,
And, from as close to the ground as possible, stares into his beloved tormentor's face.
A man plays badly yet to his own ears well enough to force the applause
Of the scowling angels he keeps on low salaries.

Sunlight twinkles through the leaves.
What is there on a day such as this that allows for a massacre,
This old man on a park bench busking for pennies,
Against whom Johann Sebastian Bach could bring a charge of murder in the first degree,
Whose mangy dog presently yowls at the skies?
Sydney could play for a thousand years, never once improve.
The angels in the branches wince.

A man hears the voice he would most like to have.
So rare, one who closes the distance between what is and would be;
All too common, one who thinks he has done so.

Sydney Housego is free of any such scruple, not for him
splitting matchsticks with an axe.
The violin was not made for a sap wearing kid gloves.
A chunk of the savage goes into making a thing fine.

A small girl in a red dress trimmed with white lace
Watches from the sanctum her childhood is, where the light
has no visible source.
If church for her is these arching trees, its priest this man
at the fiddle,
The silver collection plate is a tin can once home to a dozen
sardines.
She drops a coin there, quicksteps back to her parents who
invited her to do
What they might like to have done themselves.
The only acknowledgment she gets is
A slight nod, as much as anybody loath to interrupt the
flow of his art is prepared to concede.
Suddenly,
Mojo spotting a squirrel chases it through the bushes.
All of civilisation will not bring him to heel now.
The violin stops.
The angels make a dash for the exit, big azure skies.
Sydney whistles, then shouts the only thing any one has
heard him say for an age,
'Mojo, Mojo', as if his mouth were full of marbles, or
rather, empty of teeth.
Alas, Mojo's gone.
Sydney puts his instrument even more out of tune than
before.

The angels, bored, go back to their places in the trees.
The girl stares at the hole Mojo made in the bushes.

A harp dug up from the graves at Ur,
A sounding disc of stone from the Malayan jungle –
Should the instruments change, no matter, banjo &
clavichord are born of a single creature.
Always music comes from inside, which is how the gods
give,
Which is how one who plays only because he has to
receives.
Mojo returns, squirrelless,
So much tongue spilling out of his mouth, heavens, where
does he keep it all?
Saliva flecks Sydney's face.
If he fails to notice, not so the small girl who giggles.
The fact is, he plays just fine, better than any one has ever
done before.
The notes leap from the fiddle strings, grow invisible wings
That bear them beyond our stubborn knowledge.
The angels jabber among themselves.
We need him too, who figures this world his bench,
The smaller without whom the greater can never be.
We must now salute Sydney Housego, tap our bows,
As we make ready to perform for him this pavane.

PART TWO

Dinu Lipatti plays Chopin's Sonata in B Minor

What harmony is this?
The Tempest, III.iii.19

. . . an Hieroglyphicall and shadowed lesson
of the whole world, and [the] Creatures of God . . .
SIR THOMAS BROWNE, *Religio Medici*

Says: God the plumber comes,
A pair of oily cloth gloves, asks her what the problem is.
Answers she, the ghosts banging in the pipes, saying come,
Our heaven's a Magyar village.

Ah yes, God replies, those Chinese again.

Are you there, hello?
The woman from Budapest fumbles for a cigarette,
A slow poison the quickest cure.
Likewise, she says, the men who spread ordure with their
shoes,
As puzzled in their world as she is wise in hers,
Who go as they come, in a flowerless haze.
Sweeping up the traces, she knows better than to blame,
Says almost anything's easier than love.

She lights a thin green candle.
Appears not to notice,
Or perhaps she does, the top buttons of her blouse are
undone.

A cormorant invades the bones of her face.
She pulls a record already an antique from the battered
    sleeve,
Which she holds by the edges with reverence.
                                        Candlelight spills over its surface.

                              Says Dinu Lipatti as though the name
Were a prayer and not at all a name, she says he came as
    close
As anyone may come to music's absolute.
                                                            Listen,
As best you are able catch the small notes,
A sparrow's chatter behind a blackbird's tune,
A semiquaver in the voice, segregating false from true,
A mandolin shedding pale coins through the leaves.
So much escapes, spoils beyond our notice.
Listen, as to do so with a depth proper to the performance
Will be to compose within ourselves
An umbrella over all the newly bombed sites.
Would that he touched the random notes of my life,
Says she, her words bleeding into silence.
                                                  Are you warm enough?
Should you not be, come, sit by the candle.
A prehistoric needle drops into the groove.
A hiss at the beginning of time, band one, is a length
Of silk pulled through a hand squeezed a little, the clicks
    embers in dying fire.

                              Winter comes, the radiator explodes.
A woman alone hears things her fancy translates into images,

She would rather not say what they are.
Says one must make
Of disparate elements (ah, why not desperate?) a habitable
place.
You may pour another glass of wine.
Would you not say our wines are closer to the taste of
blood than those of France?
Says while listening to music
We should not close our eyes, or else we remove a world
not ours to remove.
If song is only sweet reverie
A fool's lulled not by love but love's perfumes.
And did not Shakespeare's couples listen with their eyes?
Where did Dante first hear light's absence?

Allegro maestoso,
We may briskly and with majesty progress to the next
course,
Says she, pushing an apple across the table.
If you were to slip the years like a robe from these
shoulders
You would find me approaching for the first time the
conservatoire,
A girl inflamed by the sounds of the instruments coming
from deep inside,
And for whom love was this, a ghostly tinkle.
What I learned was that every note in every phrase must live,
All parts give meaning to the whole.
A professor I had there, a man with a monkey's face,
Who, when I visited him to say my goodbyes,

Whispered, as though afraid his voice might carry to
another province,
Asked me whether it was not true, that music is made
solely in and through time.
I watched him peeling an apple, slowly turning the apple
Against a blade that he held perfectly still while the peel
spiralled to the floor.
I found beauty in this, as though nowhere else.
'Ah yes, Soul, of course!
Yet what's Soul,' he cried, 'without a metronome? without
Time and its sister, Space?'
'You must forgive me,' he said, 'if I tremble.'
And fool that I was, wrongly I heard a semiquaver in his
voice;
I would have to flee this poor monkey with his apple.
'Would you help me solve a riddle?'
And, with calmness approaching terror in his eyes, the old
man spoke:
'Our world bearing all the things we love
Will one day be swept like a burnt pea into space,
And the idea, the sheer audacity of it, makes me dumb
with rage.
Such are my days, punishing apathy with scales,
As though a man clutching a baton might change the
direction of the universe.
Would that it stopped there, but no, something else makes
me stare
At the alarm clock's fluorescent face.
Suppose Bach made a mistake,
Yes, the great Bach, in thinking his angelic voices

Would reach the ears of One in whom I believe and in
whom I do not believe.'
The professor soon to be emeritus dabbed his eyes.
The apple's flesh began to turn pale brown where the
afternoon sun fell at a plump angle.
'If indeed music's condition is time,
Young lady, by what powers in the cosmos can it be heard by
A God enthroned beyond time?'

Ah listen, she says, the cantabile!
An Italian scares the German out of the Pole, Bach and
Mozart his sworn guides.
What you have is Bellini, opera! One could easily drown in
waters such as these,
Yet this man who plays with reticence, sans caprice, makes
A wedding between freedom and discipline.
Would you mind if I smoke another cigarette?
Only as strong as she is fragile, she brings her face close to
the flame,
The shadows flushed out of young wrinkles.

Woman, who plays if not for your sake?

Says he was dying at the time,
So weak he had to be supported onto the stage, Dinu
Lipatti
Who played as if the pale Chopin sat by his side,
Whispering, put the *rubato* here and not where others say
it should be,
Yes, you shall be my sublunary advocate.

And so, cracking a joke between themselves, again they
    briefly live,
Whom the angels served but could not save.

You ask whether this is not miracle?
What must the world be like, O, what must we be like,
If between all that is and our crying solitude
A man with the shoulders of a wrestler plays a note
At once firm and gentle, which hanging there is also its
    opposite,
A scudding moon dressed in silence?
What are we who seek for truth in tones?
A miracle to be true asks of us not that we fall to our knees,
Only that it be worthy of our justice.

Says she has never mastered the finale.
The woman from Budapest blows out the candle,
Says playing Chopin is for her like being made love to,
She who is no man's, only music's bride.

The Charterhouse at Valldemosa

> His soul was flayed alive: a crushed rose petal,
> the shadow of a fly made him bleed.
>
> GEORGE SAND, *My Life*

I

Snow caps the pomegranate,
a buzzard drops through white
air, plucks a sparrow from the ledge.

no again no
A man pulled alive from the dream's wreckage stares.
Quickly too quickly his coming-to,
a screeching through space.

Consider where he only just was,
a salon on the Rue de la Grange-Batelière,
the chandeliers like women's voices –

Suddenly, this monk's cell with its coffin shape,
an unfinished prelude spread over the table,
a sprinkle of blood on crumpled lace.

Savage isle.

All's hell to one who seeks paradise.

2

The French lady with a manly name,
a musical Pole with an ashen face,
this couple of fools both wise
watched the steamer's phosphorescent wake.

A hand flung over the bed's edge
skims old waves.
Was it a month or a century ago
a weekly packet from Barcelona puffed for paradise,
the steersman chanting a tune?

A few drops of rain silently explode
against the windowpane.
A piano floats by, out of tune.

Majorca seeped through their eyes,
a bobbing row of windmills, skull-white,
wooden sails beckoning them ashore.

The steersman spat into the waves,
as though here's where one goes only
for squealing trade.

A man bringeth culture, pigs what he takes.

3

Wind sobs in the ravine.
A bungling of hemispheres,
a cold winter in the soul
where summer ought to be –

While others made ready to leave they came,
whom the world made gentle,
mindless of the almanac's yellowing edges,

a dead spider pressed between its pages.

A *signora* in trousers, an aura of cigar smoke,
godless,
the consumptive, burrs stuck to his town clothes –
What need have they of guidance who can afford escape?
The ascent to Valldemosa was a Spanish farce,
¡ha! an upright pulled by mules.

Aurore, my white gloves?
She and her children have already gone
to the valley for milk and potatoes.

Shivering, he pulls from the table
the pages of his unfinished prelude,
its opening phrase, D flat major, sunshine.

4

Opening bars resonant of clear skies,
though to describe them so,
and not as the azure we carry inside,

or, if pointing to where the mountain gouges
the cloud's belly,
we ask what this man's playing has to do
with things as they are,

what we do is reduce the sublime phrase
to a squeaking weathervane;
siphons we become,
through which world passes merely.

As the broken arch suggests the whole,
so these fragments he composes
are measures flung against the infinite.

A blanket wrapped about his shoulders,
sweating, he aches to be where
all things may be seen from all angles.

A single chord perhaps will find him there.

Says the C sharp major, not so.

5

So what of this woman with airs and graces,
whom Flaubert describes as
'a man who calls herself George'?

She moves with deadly innocence,
a jug of milk slopping from side to side,
a flowered bag cankered with potatoes.

Say love plays them in tones
ear does not pick up but Soul does; say love blinds her,
Revolution's child, to his *ancien régime*.

She never was for ordinary life
who, when young, kissed her father's
freshly-disinterred skull.

A few drops of rain fleck her dark and oval face.

Soon the road's barely passable.
Mud splatters her clothes
as she paddles up to
the walls of Valldemosa hidden in haze,

she who hears music in unearthly places.

6

Wet moonlight silvers the broken arches,
the monks' graves anonymous beneath the lemon trees.
Darkly he plays the same note
over and over,
watching through the music he makes
their drowned faces
staring at his from the bottom of a lake,
a waking dream so terrible
its dreamer holds himself to blame.

Suddenly, the dream plays them in reverse
so now it's he who watches
from beneath the water's surface,
icy drops from heaven

falling over where his heart is.
one by one

The door opens: she and her children shiver there,
their mouths blue,
while he jumping to his feet cries,

'Ah, I knew you were dead!'

7

A single thread of sound
                                stitches together hell and paradise,
    as precisely his now finished piece does.

She whose industry keeps them alive
                                                says, ‘Listen,
    can you not hear the dripping on the tiles?’
                                    A finger moves up and down
as if conducting from a score this one note.

                    She tells him he has composed this,
as he has already done
                                        the famished cry of an eagle,
    a guitar playing a bolero in the distance,
                          a sparrow piping beneath wet leaves.

                            ‘What, imitative harmony?’ he cries.

Anger winches him from the bottom of the lake.
                                   ‘A child slavishly follows nature,
        whereas music plays inside me.’

                    Only the furious dialogues hold true.

8

A cart thunders down the slope,
its passenger coughs blood and phlegm
beneath an almond's flowering branches.

As with everything this white plague touches
the springless vehicle is
afterwards fed to the flames.

Later, on his dying berth, he listens to
the squeals above.
All bound for pig heaven the vessel heaves,
the pink cargo slides.
The stench is unbearable.

Where's music in this?
Should we discover God here,
if only by the shape His absence makes?

Aurore, will you find for me my white gloves?

She presses a damp cloth to his face,
she whose powers to cure
are beyond her knowledge.

9

Awakes, from what, into where,
fresh linen crisp against his face,
a pillow scented with lavender.

A clock ticks in the pale corridor and, somewhere beyond,
a jury of disinfected voices
whose monotone spells assurance of a kind.
Although he's much too fastidious for existence
earth must bear him a while longer.

What music is, his life is:
a prelude that supposes what it is prelude to exists already,
if soundlessly so.

Slippered, he moves to the conservatory
where the Pleyel is,
performs what he hardly believes his.

A buzzard swoops through this high room of pearly white;
the tip of a spread wing brushes
the chandelier. It tinkles.

She at her escritoire writes,
the sound of her pen a sparrow pecking seeds at the
window ledge,
'He no longer spits up blood, sleeps well, coughs little,
and above all is in France.'

PART THREE

Communiqué for William Hoffer

Der schelchter emes is besserer vi der bester lign.
The worst truth is better than the best lie.
YIDDISH PROVERB

Bill, wicked men gnaw at their own ankles.
Our troops bivouacked at the border of silence beam
    messages
Of massive defections from the other side.
The smirkers flee, throwing their ABC's to the flames.
Slow leaves tumble, a kazoo sounds the battle charge.
We put down steel traps, calling them prizes.
All this is bright lies, our army a phantom one.
An avocado is not a grenade, but we who make it so,
Who grow rare orchids or collect wooden toys, analogize
A sterile peace from which nothing of value comes.
Meanwhile, winter creeps into the greenhouse through its
    many smashed windows.
The absurd growths within freeze.

Smallholders, we plunge deeply our stakes,
And holding our small patches of ground we lose
The world to thoughtless jackasses, spineless,
Who'd have us believe miracles come by mind alone.
They speak from a chamber of dying echoes.

Who's this squeezing a Japanese rubber ball, his
Anger which in refusing to explain itself makes us wonder
What gastric condition leads to such grimaces?

Says he just happens to be passing through. So,
Why this battle with a street map twice his size while
Trying to hold an umbrella at the same time?
A sudden gust of wind blows parks and avenues, public
monuments in his face.
Will anything ever, he cries, fold back to the old creases?
As of late he's taken to wearing loud colours,
Repeats words and phrases as if they're divinely shaped
pebbles
To be held in the mouth while meditating.
We hear wisdom, or does the stomach rumble?
We sample his cheap fare, lovers who seem to stand for lovers,
Children who seem to stand for children.
And what's this spongy thing calling itself Love?
Such words when first heard cut through the ice within
ourselves,
Only this time are spoken louder than ever before,
Capitalized, italicized . . . signifying nothing.
When do we go back to hunting real beasts with real
weapons?
Such bold language he uses, by which we mean verbs,
nouns and adjectives,
Parts of speech never grown past kittenhood.
All believing themselves prettiest they disagree with each other.
An omelette of superlatives, they make
What this shark in maroon calls style.

The soul is not as fragile as it would like to be.
Bill, the fact you are a warrior and write only in aid of
being one

Makes you invulnerable to almost anything they have.
Their old shield of protection becomes flimsy,
Weak enough to let deadly objects through.
(Will our springing you into the present tense,
As though you're still alive, make heart believe it is so?
What is our embalmer's art but making the dead seem
    about to breathe?)
A bookseller by trade, the instrument you were was delicate
Enough to pick up the faint traces of ozone
A rare book leaves in its wake, as when an electron passes
    through a cloud chamber.
So too, the words you wrote linger like perfume:
'When I attack I imagine the fire bird guides me to the
    exact centre of battle;
Of the thousands of arrows I fire
Not one fails to find its mark, but when there are no women,
    no books, no wars –
When the fire bird sleeps and there are no more enemies,
    I am unemployed utterly.'

Would you prefer we kept the news simple?
A windy night in November, which year it is matters little
Although oddly enough the hour does,
As when death came for you at precisely three in the morning.
There is a sound of crickets, although the season says no, no,
    no, impossible,
Must be the workings behind a tired man's eyes.
Questing moth looks for somewhere to settle.
Such music they make, these five lemons in a bowl of
    Prussian blue.

The furnace rumbles. Good night, forever.
A young widow in Moscow burns candles.
A soldier goes forth in the name of love.

Aurora Borealis

for George Johnston, on his 85th birthday

Who dares pick a bone with Aristotle?
The ghostly light he describes is like smoke,
A burning of straw in the countryside.

Wise Pliny made the world his catalogue,
Says when the Lacedæmonians lost Greece
An aurora mocked their galleys in flames.

The Vikings, of whom Johnston may be one,
Saw blond Valkyries swooping through battle,
Their brief to gather up the dying heroes.

What science says, a jongleur may endorse.
A solar wind brings Sun's charged particles;
They gather above earth's magnetic pole.

What happens then, the elements collide.
The electrons knocked sideways, as by love,
Warm the ions to a tremulous state.

Three pounds of starstuff childishly simple
When compared to a flickering in the nerves
Which may, with luck, translate into image.

This elderly gentleman with young eyes,
A gold wire spiralling through his earlobe,
A Viking in pale mac, speaks his verses:

Whose hat is moving on the water's face?
Alas, *poor Edward's* (stanza one, line three):
We must pray *for Edward and his trouble.*

We never get to make his acquaintance,
Yet what one watchful in his craft does is
Construct, with as few words as possible,

A sly dirge for the man of misfortune,
An asylum where he may dry his clothes.
We pity him who perhaps never was.

A dab hand, he makes his art look simple,
Although Valhalla knows the wild tumble
With the Muse, a soul covered with bruises.

While sadly he maps poor Edward's absence
The northern lights sway above our heads like
A woman sashaying down heaven's catwalk.

Whether they really do move as a whole,
Or rather, their atoms, gathering strength here
And dimming there, play upon our senses,

As they do, so dance the lords of language.

Salvatore Giuliano

Quid facies odio, sic ubi amore noces?
What will you do in your hatred, when you
  are so cruel in your love?
OVID, *Heroides*

I

We can almost smell the spent cartridges.
These gaunt figures with their wide moustaches are
  ambassadors come,
As from beyond the grave, counselling reticence,
Saying, *Speak only those words which do not hide what things
  are,*
And keep thought constantly on the move.
Who are these guns for hire, mouthing parables?
We ask them whom they serve, and, rubbing their stubble,
They hiss, *The ghost of a razor blade.*

The hills deepen with mauve,
And the bloated sun slides, bleeds over the distant pines.
The hour is all nerve.
As though piloted by some ghostly flame,
Suddenly we flare with one whom the devil in ourselves
Gave rise to, a tough who shook this isle.
What does death do with such handsome features?
A phantom of the kind engendered by dialogue
Slips between the colour of what is and the colour of what
  was,
As smoothly as a hawk on the thermal.

We debate how certain matters came to be,
And so, with a solemn measure that redeems time, we put
bare wires to
A myth dipped in formaldehyde.

All geared up to mock sleeping justice,
Our brigands prowl through the village.
They observe, while pretending not to, every move we make,
While somewhere, deep within ourselves,
We can hear their dark, tracking voices:
Psst, the gun slackly held shoots wide.

2

You wished always to be of the people,
And even though you brought them trouble
Who among them would not provide solace?
And who among them would not break the law to preserve
the code?
O Turiddu, very flesh of their silence,
You began as some Galahad on a shiny bicycle, upholding
justice.
What loser did not bask in your presence?
So who was that other who came, blasting a hole through
the haze?
Who gave shape to the darkness behind the hedge?
You were barely out of the cradle, malevolence came,
And men in their dismals began to slide.

A farmer whom misfortune drove over the edge
    sharpened his knife,
Watched the sun flash upon it, then heard the metal talk,
As talk it must have, for you saw the man smile
While he cupped his ear to the speaking blade.
A butchered snake dangled from the sacred olive tree;
Smelling the strange blood of that creature,
You thrilled to the knowledge of what makes things cease
    to be.
Pain and death absented themselves,
As though the pity of those words would make you
    hesitate.
Speed was to become a kind of virtue.
Your whole body drained with the pleasure the mule kick
Of the gun as you watched the sparrow plunge,
Although what you saw was only the slow image of
    something just gone,
An apostrophe hanging in space.
A scream flew up out of the bramble.
What it really was came from deep inside your throat,
A cry so primitive you blushed for shame.
Here, where the blood of many flows as one,
You would listen to the singing in the nerves,
And, spotting at once a false note, you'd strike as the adder
    strikes,
Without sorrow, without malice.
This, you darkly swore, the moment requires,
As to parley for but a second more would have been to see
    the hawk as dove.
The results you dumped in moonlit squares,

A note attached to each bundle, saying this one spoke,
  or that one took a bribe.
Weep, mothers and daughters and wives.
When finally the moment towered above all else, all time
  stood false.
The love you fought for, you wrapped in ice.
Your vanity was the vanity of the people,
And the photographer your only muse.

3

All day we grapple with slow commerce,
And now, with tiredness hanging upon us like shackles,
We face the dangers of the interlude.
There's everywhere the stench of failure.
Pah, spit our mild killers, cocked with pride,
Why not complain about the price of oranges?
Signori, you have not come all this distance just to lose
What by the stars above is your mandate.
You might better petition the moon than seek to communicate
  with one who rumbles in the grave.
We suggest an aspirin for your many troubles;
What remains of the night is ours to dissolve.

What stronger perfume than a just cause?
We hunger for change, and, where nothing moves, the milk
  in the dish coagulates;
A sleeping dog whimpers for the missing bone.

Such times these are, men who would aim true foul the
line,
Say honour is not what is, but what we prescribe.

4

You made crazy promises for crazy times.
A wily magician, could he have conjured hope, would have
ridden
Upon the shoulders of the populace.
A shabby god could be had at any price.
With the mood so ripe, you never slipped once.
So when did you begin to notice a drop in the temperature?
When the mammas stopped sending cakes?
The festive air of May shook with your fire.
The dead lay sprawled all over the place, their wounds
bright
As the flags which the living brought here.
Later, you would put the slaughter down to a mistake,
As though a mistake could never be a crime.
Who, then, did you suppose the people were?
Despair had begun to gnaw at your vigilance,
And, as if on purpose, you would stray into the open
spaces where
Any punk could draw a bead on fame.
You were destroyed as you deserved to be, by love.
Yes, you who would not allow the heart to meddle with
your schemes

Put faith in a man who wore white shoes.
You lay as brothers side by side, the smoke of your
cigarettes
Yellowing the white, while outside, the law would fake
the circumstances
Of your demise, as though in this place
There can be no such thing as a straight line.
You slept beneath the Judas gaze, only to awake into
death's embrace.
The news some hack had prepared well in advance sang
through the wires.
The *signora*, your mother, sank to her knees;
With the cameras clicking around her in a circle,
She pressed her lips to where you'd bled over the cobble-
stones,
Crying, *O sangue mio*.
You were already on the mortician's stone,
Bits of plaster from the death mask sticking to your face,
A player right down to the grand finale.
The *carabiniere* puzzled over your corpse,
Wondering how so much comes of so little.

Salvatore Giuliano, you may go as you please.
There is nobody here who'll divulge your crimes,
And besides, when the law frolics beneath the blanket with
the knave
What's easier than to bribe a judge?
There has been a change in the climate, too,
Which will make recognition barely possible.
The features of all we know rapidly dissolve.

What can the gelding world say of brigandage,
When young women carry guns close to themselves,
snugly as babes,
And when, instead of prayer, we place charms among the
machines?
All things high and low slide towards the middle.
There is nothing solid we can put a face to.

5

We shed by slow degrees our disquietude.
The sun edges the hills with burning magnesium white,
And the hawk shadows the creeping snake.
All things wriggle into their familiar modes.
A stallholder handles with care the dark glow of
aubergines.
A grocer scoops a pound of olives, so precise the reckoning
of hand and eye.
We find in this a deeper resonance,
A play ghosting the whole of many lives.
Any worthy thing comes, shall come, of balance.
We called him who would become resolute in hate
honourable,
And in doing so filled our house with shame.
The shutters open wide, we must go to our chores.
Our sullen desperadoes fade into the blankness of the page,
Sighing, *We shall be brought down by love*.

Uzbek Variations

for Monâjât Yultchieva

A saffron flowers on the slope.
Will you ever speak my name?

All night, sleep fled my eyes.
I warmed only frozen space.

•

A calf on a hill makes a noise,
Says, I am a full-grown mare.

A bride weeps in the house,
Says, Allah, I am a stranger.

•

Go, paint the leg of your horse
With henna my heart bleeds.

With the sinews of my life,
Sir, tie up your barking dog.

•

Quickly man destroys the house
Whose beams he put up with care.

She who prays he might change
Scrubs the raven's wing white.

•

Wash me with flowered water,
Sew me into a shroud of leaves.

May these tears the wind blows
Wet the blossom of your face.

NOTES

TIGER MUSIC: The poem owes much, including several phrases, to a chapter in Marmaduke Pickthall's *Oriental Encounters* (1904). I was informed by my friend Subhi in Damascus that in Arabic there are sixty-seven words for 'lion'; I assume, perhaps wrongly, that there must be almost as many for 'tiger'.

A SEVENTH JEW: This poem has its origins in an incident that came to light during the Klaus Barbie trial. Seven members of the French Resistance in Lyon were arrested, imprisoned, and shortly afterwards executed; we know the identities of six of the people but of the seventh only that he was Jewish and that before being taken from his cell to be shot he sang Mario Cavaradossi's aria from Act III of Puccini's *Tosca*. The opening lines of the poem draw from an uncredited translation of the libretto.

DINU LIPATTI PLAYS CHOPIN'S SONATA IN B MINOR: The Romanian pianist, Dinu Lipatti (1917–1950), was famously described by Walter Legge as having 'the shoulders of a wrestler'. The few recordings he made are, in almost every instance, considered by many to be 'definitive' readings of the works he chose. These performances are all the more remarkable because Lipatti was already suffering terribly from the cancer that would soon take his life. There are a couple of lines in the poem that draw from Walter Legge's article on Lipatti in the February 1951 issue of *Gramophone* magazine. Certain of the musical ideas and a phrase or two owe their existence to Victor Zuckerkandl's *Sound and Symbol, Music and the External World* (Routledge & Kegan Paul, 1956).

THE CHARTERHOUSE AT VALLDEMOSA: George Sand, born Aurore Dupin, and the consumptive Frédéric Chopin went to Majorca in the autumn of 1838 hoping to find there an improving climate, and over three months experienced what was to be one of the island's coldest winters in decades. That Chopin survived at all was due to George Sand's diligence and common sense. Ill though he was, Chopin managed to complete his remarkable *24 Preludes*, op. 28. The odd circumstances behind the composition of the so-called 'Raindrop Prelude', no. 15, in D flat major, are recounted in Sand's memoirs, *Histoire de ma vie* (1848), and it is from this work and her account of their stay at the almost deserted Carthusian monastery at Valldemosa, *Un Hiver à Majorque* (1840), that I have drawn several apt phrases. The closing lines of the poem are from a letter written by Sand, on February 26th, 1839, to Charlotte Marliani.

COMMUNIQUÉ FOR WILLIAM HOFFER: William Hoffer (1944–1997). 'There are many of us who looked upon Bill Hoffer as a cross between a subversive philosopher, an unfulfilled bookseller and some kind of genius,' wrote Paul Minet in an obituary of him. Certainly, he was one of the best poets not to have written verse. Exasperated with the Canadian literary scene, whose fiercest critic he was, he closed his bookshop in Vancouver and moved to Moscow. A man with his hair combed back, he said, always looks as if he is going somewhere. After announcing, late one night, on a crackling telephone line, his abandonment of the English language he married a Russian, Masha Averyanova, with whom he collected some four thousand wooden toys. The poem is a collaboration with its subject who, really, has no choice in the matter. I have pulled a number of lines from his letters to me and from another, a small masterpiece of invective, which he wrote to a poet whose several volumes he particularly disliked. The military terminology is in no small measure a nod towards Hoffer's own use of the same, particularly in his rôle of Commander in Chief of TANKS, not so much a publishing venture as a one-man *zeitgeist*. I have never grown orchids.

AURORA BOREALIS: The italicized passages are from George Johnston's poem 'Poor Edward' first published in his collection *The Cruising Auk* (Oxford University Press, Toronto, 1959).

SALVATORE GIULIANO: 'Sicily is a metaphor for the modern world' – Leonardo Sciascia. Salvatore 'Turridu' Giuliano (1922–1950) was arguably the last Sicilian bandit worthy of note, although any greatness we might attribute to him is diminished by the folly of some of his ambitions. Among the most impractical of these was that Sicily be made the 49th American state, a proposal to which President Truman did not rise. With over a hundred slayings attached to his name, Giuliano may have had some hankering for a cause. I have composed nothing of biographical value here. A somewhat glamorized, though properly inclusive, account of his life may be found in Gavin Maxwell's *God Protect Me From My Friends* (Longman, Green and Co., London, 1956), and a more rigorously investigated one in Billy Jaynes Chandler's *King of the Mountain* (Northern Illinois University Press, DeKalb, 1988). As must always be the case, no one book about a bandit and his ambiguities can satisfy whole. Among the problems hardest to resolve is Giuliano's part in the shooting down of men, women and children at an outdoor Communist rally, the infamous Portella della Ginestra incident, although, to give him his say, he claimed to have been unaware of what took place. In true bandit fashion, Giuliano was betrayed by his close friend, Gaspare Pisciotta, but mystery still surrounds the circumstances. There is no hard evidence that Gaspare ever wore white shoes, and, among other liberties the poem takes, the ghostly gang which stalks its pages bears no resemblance to any persons dead or alive. The sacrifice of the snake is an ancient, presumably pagan, Sicilian charm against crop failure.

UZBEK VARIATIONS: Several of the lines are adaptations from translations of Persian poetry, more specifically those heard in the songs of the Sufi singer, Monâjât Yultchieva, and printed in the booklet accompanying her recording *Ouzbekistan* (Ocora/Radio France C 560060).

Ivan V. Lalić

A Rusty Needle

Fading Contact

TRANSLATED BY FRANCIS R. JONES

Gabriel Levin

Ostraca

Federico García Lorca

A Season in Granada

EDITED AND TRANSLATED BY CHRISTOPHER MAURER

Thomas McCarthy

Mr Dineen's Careful Parade

NEW AND SELECTED POEMS

Dennis O'Driscoll

Weather Permitting

POETRY BOOK SOCIETY RECOMMENDATION

Vasko Popa

Collected Poems

TRANSLATED BY ANNE PENNINGTON

AND FRANCIS R. JONES

Sally Purcell

Fossil Unicorn

Daniel Weissbort

What Was All the Fuss About?